AF408424

Copy right ©2022 Vincent Cven

All Right Reserved

No part of this book should be republish
in any form without permission from the rightful
owner. Be ware of copyrights infringement.

Quotes piece
Of -cvenswrites

Vincent Cven
a.k.a
-cvenswrites

Cvens

-CVENSWRITES

We may be familiar with using quotation in support to what we are saying or trying to convey to an individual. Quotes piece of -cvenswrites is the original intellect quotes of the author created out of thoughts and the words that could conceal behind it a better understanding.

-CVENSWRITES

(20) MOTIVATIONAL QUOTES
PIECE OF -CVENSWRITES

-CVENSWRITES

- If others can make it successfully
you are not exceptional.

-cvenswrites

- Remember there are gloomy days
and still the brightest days, if you fail
today, you can still make it successfully
huge in another day.

-cvenswrites

-If they doubt you,react to them
just by showing more efforts to
your work that you are believing
yourself for.

-cvenswrites

- Remember there are gloomy days
and still the brightest days, if you fail
today, you can still make it successfully
huge in another day.

-cvenswrites

- In all things, you should be
yourself biggest fan. There's
no reason to depends on others
support at first moves.

-cvenswrites

- Loser loses and give up.
Winner loses and press on.

-cvenswrites

- Over work yourself now
so in the future, you would
only have less to put in to
work .

-cvenswrites

- If you have ,fail not to give
to those in need. Believe me,
there's blessings attached to
helping the needy.

-cvenswrites

-CVENSWRITES

- Be active to build your visions
now that you are younger. So in
older age you would have more
to eat.

-cvenswrites

- You are the leader for everything
you're believing yourself to
accomplish for.

-cvenswrites

- When you get an hateful speech
or comment for whatever you have
put out there from your creativity, just
know that's the moment they have taken
notice of you.. So Don't give up and show
to them what you've got .

-cvenswrites

-cVENSWRITES

- knowledge is constant. Don't feel
you Know it all and always be willing
to listen to whatever anyone has to say
to acquire more knowledge.

-cvenswrites

- Don't forget where you are coming from,
no matter where you get to be today.
That's part of what made you today.

-cvenswrites

- If it's hard or painful today, just know
that tomorrow it will be easy and less
painful.

-cvenswrites

- Those famous people and celebrity
you see today and admired, remember
they were once like you and so if you
want to make it bigger like them, it's not
impossible just it would require you not
to give up.

-cvenswrites

-cvenswrites

- If you are feeling like giving up,
remember your aim and it's
outcome and just trust yourself
as you did before starting it up
at the first place. You will feel
better.

-cvenswrites

- Just know that you are a survival,
because no matter how hard it is in
the world today. We are all still alive .

-cvenswrites

-CVENSWRITES

-We are all stars. it's up to you
if you choose to shine the brightest
among the brighter ones.

-cvenswrites

- If you fail, atleast you tried
-if you give up, it's okay you lose
-But if you keep on, it's assured
you can still win.

-cvenswrites

-They may not like what you have to present.
But believe me, there are still millions standing
on the line and waiting for more of what you have
to present.. (But you will see these millions when you
Don't give up)

-cvenswrites

-cvenswrites

(20) DARK QUOTES
PIECE OF -CVENSWRITES

-CVENSWRITES

Hell is alive..
It's living among
us all.

-cvenswrites

- It's easy to kiss
the devil when you
are busy with sins.

-cvenswrites

-Snakes are more quiet
that's why you can't tell
when they strike.

-cvenswrites

- Snakes are better
hunters.

-cvenswrites

- There's no hope,
if you can't create
an opportunity..

   -cvenswrites

- dark is better when
you feel the urge to do
something nasty.

   -cvenswrites

- lips runs faster when they are lying.
Heart beats faster reminding you that
you are guilty.

-cvenswrites

- Sin is contagious and
its endemic in every society.

-cvenswrites

- blood cries and dies
when it's forced out of the
flesh where it's meant to be.

-cvenswrites

- life gives you an option
You choose between.

-cvenswrites

- In the dark and rainy weather
every girl is sweeter..

-cvenswrites

- Both God and Devil
resides in every human.
It depends on what part they
choose to live mostly with .

-cvenswrites

-when you kiss the
edge, it may hurt but
at least you could now
be experienced.

-cvenswrites

You will never understand
until you get to be experienced.

-cvenswrites

-The dark gives the
stars the opportunity
to shine..

-cvenswrites

-Devil get you prepared
and will leave you when he's
done.

-cvenswrites

-Death doesn't need an
invitation card to be invited.

-cvenswrites

- Actually, when a fool is
rich he feels he doesn't need
the correction.

-cvenswrites

- In every man's life,
comes a time death
would surely knock at
his door.

-cvenswrites

- Weak soul gives his self
a righteous reason to sin.

-cvenswrites

(20) LIFE QUOTES
PIECE OF -CVENSWRITES

-CVENSWRITES

-The color of life
is green.

-cvenswrites

-CVENSWRITES

- If you aren't wisen up
you may end up being
kicked out of the game
of living.

-cvenswrites

-If you understand the
ladders of life, there's
possibility you will
live longer..

-cvenswrites

-CVENSWRITES

- Life is simply filled
in with two contradictory.
It's up to you whichever
you choose..

-cvenswrites

-There are so many folds
that needs to be unfolded
with time as you keep going
through the steps of living...

-cvenswrites

- life is health, when you know
how to maintain it. However,
life can be hell if you choose
to run faster than you should.

-cvenswrites

-Life is a movie.
God is the creator.
We are the actors.
Parents are the producers.

-cvenswrites

-Life helps you when you can
maintain it's environment..

-cvenswrites

-Being alive works very
closer with the time clock..

-cvenswrites

- Learn to mingle, because you
aren't made to be single..

-cvenswrites

- If there's no pain, sadness,
down moment, you are likely
not to fully understand life.

-cvenswrites

- Life is in the air, and everything
you can see, touch and feel
around you..

-cvenswrites

- Life doesn't show you it's
sweet part easily, you work
to earn it.

-cvenswrites

-Life dies when you see it
brown like a scorched leaf..

-cvenswrites

- Appreciate what we call life
when it's not at it's worse to you.
You will find more reason to live.

   -cvenswrites

-If you can complete your chapters
of life with no more bad acts, you
are likely to score 1hundred percent
of your entire story once more.

   -cvenswrites

- Life would always give you
an option to choose from.

-cvenswrites

-Being alive is attached
to the elements of (Air)
and (Water).

-cvenswrites

- The name life is in
the street..

-cvenswrites

-Don't forget to smile because
It's important to the health of
being alive.

-cvenswrites

(20) QUOTES PIECE FOR HOPE OF -CVENSWRITES

-CVENSWRITES

You only make hope available
for yourself, when you choose
to believe and have faith.

-cvenswrites

Hope is alive among
positive vibes.

-cvenswrites

Negativity makes it hard
for you to sense the presence
of hope and positivity.

-cvenswrites

Hope is only of the living.
That's what the dead are
deprived of.

-cvenswrites

Faith, believing and
hope all stroll together..

-cvenswrites

Hopefulness is what most
would cling to.

-cvenswrites

Hope gives us reason
to keep living..

-cvenswrites

Dead hope is as a result
of dead faith.

-cvenswrites

Depression kills the presence of hope
Doubt over shadows hope.

-cvenswrites

Hope is in our every day
lives. It's up to us to take
the opportunity.

-cvenswrites

If you can keep trying, then
there's Hope for you.

.

-cvenswrites

Don't threaten hope.
It may leave your side
for certain period of time,
Could be longer or short time
.. but at least it won't be forever.

-cvenswrites

Sin hides hope from us.
Realizing it, gives us hope,
to be forgiven.

.

-cvenswrites

-CVENSWRITES

Hope is attached to the amount
of time you put in achieving a
certain goal some day .

-cvenswrites

Don't look down at anyone,
because you may not know
when hope will manifest it'self
to them.

.

-cvenswrites

Hope never dies,if
you keep believing .

-cvenswrites

Hope is not selective.
It manifest more to those
who believe in what it has
to present to them and they
keep trying.

.

-cvenswrites

Hope is actually alive .

-cvenswrites

Hope is a comforter of an
over thinking mind, because
it tells you that all will be alright
someday..

-cvenswrites

-CVENSWRITES

Hope will always come to your
heart Knocking... It's up to you
to believe it or doubt it.

-cvenswrites

(20) PSYCHOLOGICAL
QUOTES PIECE OF
,-CVENSWRITES

-CVENSWRITES

-The mind speaks when
you pay attention to it.

-cvenswrites

-The soul is the spirit of the body.
The mind is the spirit of the heart
and brain.

-cvenswrites

-What you allow to fill your
mind, that it gives to your
body.

-cvenswrites

-The mind is at peace, when
there's no guilty eating it up..

-cvenswrites

-The mind is the spirit
of the memory.

-cvenswrites

- Every mentality varies base
on knowledge.

-cvenswrites

-87% percent of the mind
is still locked towards the
knowledge of things beyond.

-cvenswrites

- The mind gives you an idea,
It's up to you to carry it out or
not.

-cvenswrites

- Sin is the virus that
invades the mind.

   -cvenswrites

-You cleans your mind
through deep thought and
breath.

   -cvenswrites

- The mind does die when the
flesh dies, It's still alive as long as
the soul is still roaming..

-cvenswrites

-Mindsets is what makes the
different social class.

-cvenswrites

-Sensibilty matters more,
even without knowledge
but then you will notice that
you can't be sensible when
there's no wisdom and knowledge.

-cvenswrites

-If you trigger the psychological
part, you will understand that it's
more dangerous.

-cvenswrites

-Mentality is another Power
that keeps a man in order..

-cvenswrites

- Weak mind, grows quicker ego.

.

-cvenswrites

-Heart will be broken.
Eyes will shed tears.
Foot would move on.
Mind will keep every record...

-cvenswrites

- The mind is the box of
what the body goes through.

-cvenswrites

-Mental age is different
from your actual age.

-cvenswrites

-YOU grow earlier when you
keep faster RECORDS to your
mind than what your age
should handle.

.

-cvenswrites

(20) BELIEVERS QUOTE
PIECE OF -CVENSWRITES

- Believing what's yet to come but not yet present is a stronger belief.

-cvenswrites

-Believers have unshakable Faith.

-cvenswrites

- Even in the darkest moment
the heart of a believer still shine
more because they are never over
shadowed by the dangers before them.

-cvenswrites

-Every violent storm will still be calm.
The scorching sun will still melt off.
That's the heart of a believer.

-cvenswrites

- Hope is the believer's
best reminder.

-cvenswrites

-Goodness and happiness will
always be the last end of every
pain.

-cvenswrites

- we are all stars...
You can choose to shine bright
or even the brightest.

-cvenswrites

- pain will be taken away
and there will be so many fruits
to bear.

-cvenswrites

- giving up and keeping on
are both alternatives to choose
from.

-cvenswrites

- There's an answer to every mystery
.

-cvenswrites

- Days will be gloomy because
the rainbow is coming.

-cvenswrites

- The heart has no eyes to see
but feels. And so, you shouldn't
see to believe but as long as it feels
right from your heart.

.

-cvenswrites

- keep trying because it would
 just take one day to win..

    -cvenswrites

- Tears will still dry up and
   there will be smile.

    -cvenswrites

-Hope never dies for
the living.

-cvenswrites

Even the sky knows
it's going to be alright.

-cvenswrites

-Every effort is never a waste.
It teaches a lesson or bring out
an anticipated result..

-cvenswrites

- There are colorful fruits
in every steps of life when
accomplished.

-cvenswrites

-Every steps you take, takes
you in further levels from the
place you use to be..

-cvenswrites

- keep on, you are
surely heading somewhere
higher.

-cvenswrites

(20) CHRISTAIN QUOTE
PIECE OF -CVENSWRITES

-CVENSWRITES

- Believe that it is done in
accordance as you have prayed
for.

-cvenswrites.

-It worth more
having faith.

-cvenswrites

- A tiny sin could ruin your entire life.
But, forgiveness is always available .

-cvenswrites.

-If you choose to sin,
you are pushing God
away.

-cvenswrites

- Just be good and righteous,
  For that is wisdom .

     -cvenswrites.

-There is no excusable sin.

     -cvenswrites

- There will certainly be peace
after what we have now in the
world .

-cvenswrites.

-Knowledge is wisdom
and wisdom means knowing
God and understanding his
ways.

-cvenswrites

- The good people will attract good.
  The bad ones will attract bad .

     -cvenswrites.

-Its better to be spiritually active
because alot of things goes on
in the spirit realm before it's manifest
in the real world.

     -cvenswrites

- The heart never lies.

-cvenswrites.

- Flesh is weaker than the
spirit.

-cvenswrites

- Miracle happens.
But some requires you to
put an effort in doing something
for miracle to manifest..

-cvenswrites.

- Blessed soul is more at peace
when it remains righteous.

-cvenswrites

- Earth is our resident home,
    (not permanent)..

    -cvenswrites.

- Miracle happens when you
    don't expect it.

    -cvenswrites

- The bible is our manual guide.
Prayer is our contact call.
Faith is our assurance.

-cvenswrites.

- There are billons of lives on
this Earth, be assured that God
is working on your own miracle.

-cvenswrites

- A prayer less believer
is more likely to fall victim..

-cvenswrites.

-CVENSWRITES

- The only thing physically
you can connect to God
with is the Bible. The rest
requires emotionally and
spiritual .

-cvenswrites

-CVENSWRITES

-CVENSWRITES
@vinpoemlyri

-CVENSWRITES

www.ingramcontent.com/pod-product-compliance
Lightning Source LLC
Chambersburg PA
CBHW081916120726
47996CB00010B/3356